CW00735482

SAAB 35
DRAKEN

SAAB 35 DRAKEN

Scandinavian 'Cold War' Warrior

Jan Jorgensen

Airlife
England

A close formation of four different SAAB aircraft designs; the SAAB 105 jet trainer (SK60 F5-49) followed by the SAAB 32 Lansen (A32A FC-28), SAAB 35 Draken (J35F FC-19) and SAAB 37 Viggen (JA37 FC-48) fighters. *(Author)*

Acknowledgements

Now entering its twilight years, the distinctive and attractive SAAB 35 Draken is a real fighter pilot's aeroplane. With its remaining users the Draken is extraordinarily popular, and its narrow but comfortable cockpit is still a sought-after position. Pilots of the Draken community are justifiably proud of remaining competitive in their workload-intensive but rewarding hot rods.

For the author, the Draken has always been a fascinating aircraft, and over the last ten years he has amassed a large collection of photographs showing all aspects of Draken operations. However, a few good friends have also contributed with photographs for this book, and special thanks for both large and small contributions go to Peter Foster, Cor van Gent, Wolfgang Hainzl, Steen Hartov, Jyrki Laukkanen, Anders Nylén, Douglas Sloviak and Lutz Tonne.

The author would also like to express his sincere thanks to all officers and aircrews for their generous hospitality and support when providing photographic facilities. Without their assistance this book would not have been possible.

Copyright © 1997 Jan Jorgensen

First published in the UK in 1997 by Airlife Publishing Ltd

British Library Cataloguing-in Publication Data
A catalogue record for this book is available from the British Library

ISBN 1 85310 729 8

All rights reserved. No part of this book may be reproduced or transmitted in any form or by any means, electronic or mechanical including photo-copying, recording or by any information storage and retrieval system, without permission from the Publisher in writing.

Typeset by Phoenix Typesetting, Ilkley, West Yorkshire

Printed in Hong Kong

Airlife Publishing Ltd
101 Longden Road, Shrewsbury, SY3 9EB, England

Introduction

Since it was founded on 2 April 1937, Swedish aviation company SAAB (*Svenska Aeroplan Aktiebolaget*) has developed and produced more than 4,000 aircraft of 13 different types, most of them specially tailored to meet Swedish Air Force requirements. Because of Sweden's long-standing policy of armed neutrality, the nation has developed a very competent aviation industry that, more or less independent of foreign technology, produces advanced aircraft designs for Sweden's military forces. For more than 50 years SAAB has manufactured all of the major aircraft and missile types for the Swedish Air Force, and today Sweden is probably the world's smallest nation still capable of developing modern combat aircraft equal to the most advanced fighters designed by the world's largest nations.

The company's first products were the propeller-driven SAAB 17 single-engine and SAAB 18 twin-engine bombers, as well as the SAAB 21 twin-boom fighter and its SAAB 21R jet successor. Then came the SAAB 90 Scandia transport and SAAB 91 Safir light trainer, later followed by the SAAB 105 jet trainer and SAAB 340 regional airliner. But it was the development of a long series of distinctive combat aircraft such as the SAAB 29 Tunnan, SAAB 32 Lansen, SAAB 35 Draken, SAAB 37 Viggen and SAAB 39 Gripen that really established SAAB's reputation for producing outstanding world-class aeroplanes.

Characteristically, SAAB engineers have never been afraid of stretching their imagination and choosing unconventional design solutions when trying to meet project specifications and improve aircraft performance. This was the case in the autumn of 1949, when a young and innovative aircraft designer, SAAB project manager Erik Bratt, started working on Project 1250(R), which eventually evolved into the distinctive SAAB 35 Draken supersonic fighter. Bratt developed the unique, and at that time very advanced double-delta wing configuration to combine good high-speed performance at altitude (Mach 2+) with exceptional low-speed manoeuvrability for short take-off and landing distances (about 500 m).

Initial wind tunnel experiments quickly confirmed that Bratt's paper-generated conclusions were accurate. The double-delta wing had lower supersonic drag than a conventional swept wing and better CG versus CL positions than a pure delta wing. To gain some practical experience with the new and unproven double-delta configuration, Bratt's team decided to take the project out of the wind tunnel and into the sky.

A series of wire-controlled, pulsejet-powered scale models about one metre long were constructed and flown extensively to explore various design configurations. It is even rumoured that preliminary double-delta testing was conducted by the team members eagerly flying hand-launched paper models in their offices at SAAB in Linköping!

As the project gradually moved further ahead a 70% scale experimental piloted aircraft was constructed and flown for the first time on 21 January 1952. This aerodynamic testbed was designated the SAAB 210, but because of its characteristic planform it quickly became nicknamed the 'Draken' (Dragon), and later 'Lill-Draken' (Little Dragon) as the fully-fledged fighter took over the Draken name. It was used to explore the effect of various modifications to the nose, intake and wing, as well as for gathering data on general double-delta handling characteristics. After a total of 887 successful flights, totalling 286 hr, the SAAB 210 was retired and the project design configuration frozen.

The first SAAB 35 Draken prototype, serial 35-1 was flown for the first time on 25 October 1955, with SAAB test pilot Bengt R. Olow at the controls. Initially three prototypes were constructed, but the entire Draken programme eventually involved 13 prototypes of different versions. For two years the prototypes continued to explore and expand the flight envelope before, on 15 February 1958, the first production-standard J35A (serial 35-5) made its maiden flight. Important Draken milestones were achieved on 26 January 1956, when one of the SAAB 35 prototypes exceeded Mach 1.0, and on 14 January 1960, when a production J35B reached Mach 2.0.

SAAB 35 production was kept running for more than two decades, a total of 615 Drakens being constructed in 12 different versions and delivered to the air forces of four nations. The SAAB 35 had remarkable development potential, and within its basic Draken planform the type evolved from supersonic interceptor through photo-reconnaissance to tactical attack, doubling its maximum take-off weight from 8 to 16 tonnes in the process but still maintaining excellent performance. Today, an estimated 200 Drakens are still flying worldwide.

Main Draken operator

OPPOSITE PAGE:
An underside view of a J35F, showing its distinctive double-delta planform and the squadron badge of 1.div/F10 (a ghost) below the inner wings. The leading-edge sweep-back angle of the inboard wing section is 80 degrees and of the outboard section 57 degrees. The thickness-to-chord ratio is 5%. The outer wing is easily removable for road transport, reducing the aircraft's width to only 4.40 m. Note that the rear part of the fuselage underside is left unpainted natural metal, a normal practice on *Flygvapnet* Drakens because the paint cannot withstand the heat from the RM6C engine which, with an overall length of more than 8 m (55% occupied by the afterburner), often is referred to as 'the world's longest jet engine'.
(Anders Nylén)

SAAB J35F callsign *Johan Röd 57* makes a climbing left turn high above a massive cloud cover. Fighters in *Flygvapnet* service normally use tactical radio callsigns which identify the individual aircraft as follows: the wing number is indicated by the name of the corresponding letter in the Swedish phonetic alphabet (which is *Johan* for F10, being the name for the 10th letter). The squadron number is indicated by a colour, with the squadrons within a Wing always being allocated colours as follows: *Röd* (red) for 1st Division, *Blå* (blue) for 2nd Division and *Gul* (yellow) for 3rd Division. Finally, the individual aircraft tailcode number is used. Thus, radio callsign *Johan Röd 57* identifies the aircraft as tailcode 57 of 1.div/F10 (= J35F c/n 35559).
(Anders Nylén)

The initial Drakens delivered to the *Svenska Flygvapnet* (Swedish Air Force) in March 1960 were soon superseded by much-improved versions, and SAAB has repeatedly switched production to new and better models or carried out extensive modifications to older airframes. Draken variants in *Flygvapnet* service have included the J35A, J35B, J35D, J35F and J35J (J for *Jakt*, or interception), Sk35C (Sk for *Skol*, or training) and S35E (S for *Spaning*, or reconnaissance).

For many years the SAAB 35 Draken has constituted the backbone of Swedish air defence, and it still maintains a vital cornerstone in *Flygvapnet* combat readiness. At the height of its career, in the late 1960s and early 1970s, Drakens of various sub-types equipped no fewer than 26 *Divisioner* (squadrons) organised within 11 *Flottiljer* (Wings).

With delivery of the potent SAAB JA37 Viggen interceptor from 1979 onwards and a general reduction in the number of fighter units, only the *Skånska Flygflottilj*, F10, at Ängelholm continues to operate two *Divisioner* of the ultimate J35J Draken interceptor as well as the Sk35C two-seat trainer. Since 1994 F10 has also operated one *Division* equipped with the SAAB AJS37 Viggen attack and reconnaissance version. Based in the extreme south-western corner of Sweden, F10 plays an important role within *Flygvapnet* command structure as a so-called *Sektor-Flygflottilj* (Sector Wing), being responsible for one of three Air Defence Sectors which together cover surveillance and control of the entire Swedish airspace.

The *Södra Luftforsvarssektorn* (Air Defence Sector South) is commanded by the F10 Wing Chief and controls all interceptor components within its specified operational area, which in addition to F10 comprises F17 at Ronneby with two *Divisioner* of SAAB JA37 Viggen. Also at the commander's disposal are a large number of well dispersed reserve air bases (usually five for each Wing) and a semi-automatic surveillance and control system including a network of operation centres, radar stations, optical observation posts and extensive communications.

The Draken is expected to continue in *Flygvapnet* service until F10 converts to the new SAAB JAS39 Gripen multi-role combat aircraft around year 2000.

Drakens of 3.div/F10 J35J on patrol off the Swedish west coast, not far from their home base at Ängelholm. (Anders Nylén)

Specially painted J35F F10-62 (c/n 35586), callsign *Johan Gul 62*, somewhere over southern Sweden. Note the large swordfish, the squadron badge of 3.div/F10, painted on top and below the wings, and the excessive use of yellow, which is the squadron colour of the 3rd Division. *(Anders Nylén)*

An impressive shot of J35J F10-24 (c/n 35624) of the 3rd Division, callsign *Johan Gul 24*, banking low over the sound between Sweden and Denmark, carrying four 525 litre drop tanks and a pair of Rb24J Sidewinder missiles. The J35J (and the now-retired S35E reconnaissance version) are the only *Flygvapnet* Drakens which can carry four drop tanks, giving an extra 2,100 litres of fuel which almost doubles the J35J's internal fuel capacity of 2,865 litres. The wing pylons were not tubed for fuel on other *Flygvapnet* Draken versions, meaning, for example, the J35F can carry only two drop tanks on its underfuselage stations. *(Anders Nylén)*

SAAB Sk35C Draken trainer F10-87 (c/n 35810) manoeuvring hard somewhere over southern Sweden. All Sk35Cs have been converted from early production J35A airframes initially constructed in 1960–61, and therefore they are the oldest Drakens still flying anywhere today. Note that the '*Cäsar*' version carries only a single 525-litre drop tank on its central underfuselage station. Also clearly visible are the extra fins mounted under the outer wings to compensate for the larger vertical area of the two-seat cockpit. *(Anders Nylén)*

9

A pair of *Flygflottilj 10* J35J Drakens bank
right in close formation, carrying a standard
combat-mix weapon load of two infrared
(IR) homing Rb24J Sidewinders on the inner
wing pylons and two semi-active radar-
guided Rb27 Falcons on the outer wing
pylons, plus two 525-litre drop tanks on the
underfuselage stations. *(Anders Nylén)*

A Draken pilot 'on the job' in his J35J. Despite the Draken's age, its cockpit is still a sought-after position for young *Flygvapnet* fighter pilots, who prize the aircraft's performance, agility and high workload. You cannot just sit and enjoy the ride in a Draken, you have to be ahead of it mentally and in full control all the time. The Draken is demanding and unforgiving; it can accelerate to supersonic speed in a few seconds, but it can just as quickly reduce its speed to almost zero and end up in a superstall if you pull a higher angle of attack than your speed allows. You have to be good to fly a Draken, whereas the newer Viggen is perhaps more forgiving, easier to fly, and less demanding to operate. *(Anders Nylén)*

SAAB J35J Draken F10-27 (c/n 35627) cruising straight and level high in the Swedish sky. Powered by a Volvo Flygmotor RM6C afterburning turbofan (a licence-built Rolls-Royce Avon 300 with a Swedish developed Model 67 afterburner), the Draken has a thrust-to-weight ratio of 0.70 in normal air-to-air configuration, improving to 0.85 if only 50% fuel is carried. *(Anders Nylén)*

A J35J F10-56 (c/n 35556) on finals for landing at its Ängelholm base. This view gives a good impression of the Draken's unique four-point undercarriage arrangement, featuring a steerable (by cockpit-mounted tiller wheel) forward retracting nose gear unit, two outward retracting main gear assemblies (hydraulically shortened during the retraction cycle to permit stowage in the undercarriage bays), and a rearward retracting tailwheel bumper unit. The special tailwheel became necessary with the introduction of the lengthened Model 66 (and later Model 67) afterburner unit from the 66th production J35A onwards, which gave better performance at high altitude. The improved afterburner was some 75 cm longer than the original Model 65 unit, demanding a redesign of the rear fuselage section and adoption of an extended tailcone with a tailwheel assembly to prevent damage due to over-rotation on take-off or excessive angle of attack on landing. *(Anders Nylén)*

A lone *Flygflottilj 10* J35J Draken approaches the Swedish west coast at low level on its way back to Ängelholm. The Draken's double-delta wing trailing edge has move-able control surfaces extending across virtually the full span, four elevon segments (two on each wing) operating in unison for pitch control and differentially for roll control. Actuation of the elevons (and the rudder) is accomplished hydraulically, and is integrated with a three-axis automatic stability unit which provides artificial feel for the pilot's control column and rudder pedals. *(Anders Nylén)*

A nice line-abreast formation of four Sk35C Draken trainers. On average, the *Flygvapnet* requires five to ten new Draken drivers per year, but in addition Austrian pilots receive TIS-35 training at Ängelholm (which Sweden is committed to provide under the contract signed in 1985, when Austria purchased 24 refurbished SAAB 35OE fighters). At present, nine Sk35Cs remain in F10 service, each of which has some 200 flying hours left of its structural lifetime. This is estimated to be sufficient for the rest of the Draken's active years in *Flygvapnet*. *(Anders Nylén)*

OPPOSITE TOP:
A nice formation showing all three SAAB Draken versions operated by *Flygflottilj 10* at Ängelholm during the early 1990s; from front to rear: J35F F10-66 (c/n 35468) of 1.div/F10, Sk35C F10-85 (c/n 35817) of 1.div/F10 and J35J F10-39 (c/n 35539) of 2.div/F10. *(Anders Nylén)*

OPPOSITE BOTTOM:
Three J35F and three Sk35C marked with the red and white ghost badge of the 1st Division of *Flygflottilj 10* at Ängelholm flying a delta formation in the beautiful late afternoon sunlight of the Nordic winter. *(Anders Nylén)*

SAAB J35F callsign *Johan Röd 66*, F10-66 (c/n 35468), of *Skånska Flygflottilj* with a specially painted fin displaying the famous ghost squadron badge of 1st Division from *Flygflottilj 10* at Ängelholm. This is the oldest insignia in Swedish military aviation history, as 1.div/F10 can trace its ghost badge back to the Second World War, fully living up to the squadron motto: 'The show must go on'. In 1994 this unit converted to the AJS37 Viggen, leaving the 2nd and 3rd Divisions of F10 as the only remaining SAAB 35 Draken operators in *Flygvapnet* service. *(Author)*

This J35F flying inverted on full afterburner clearly shows the Draken's characteristic double-delta wing planform. Developed by SAAB during the 1950s, this unique geometry combined good high-speed performance at altitude (Mach 2+) with exceptional low-speed manoeuvrability and short take-off and landing distances (about 500 m). A less attractive feature of the double-delta concept was the so-called superstall, a phenomenon of delta wings when the angle of attack is too high. *(Author)*

SAAB J35F-2 Draken FC-19 (c/n 35519) of the *Försökscentralen* (FC-Test Centre) at Malmslätt approaches for touchdown. The FC operates examples of most Swedish military aircraft and helicopter types, and is tasked with the development and evaluation of all aviation related equipment and tactics for the Swedish Army (*Armén*), Navy (*Marinen*) and Air Force (*Flygvapnet*). *(Author)*

Newly modified all-grey J35J Draken F10-62 (c/n 35586) of *Skånska Flygflottilj* at Ängelholm. To extend the operational life of its remaining Draken fleet well into the 1990s, *Flygvapnet* decided in 1985 to modify and refurbish a batch of 66 low-houred J35Fs into a new version, the J35J. In addition to these, a single J35J prototype conversion was thoroughly evaluated by the *FC* at Malmslätt before the modernisation programme, initially known as *System 35 Ny*, was carried out by SAAB and FFV Aerotech in 1987–91. All J35J *'Johan'* updates were drawn from J35F-2 *'Filip-Två'* airframes (the J35F with an undernose IR sensor) while most J35F-1 *'Filip-Ett'* Drakens (without the undernose IR sensor) have now been withdrawn from use. *(Author)*

When *Flygflottilj 18* at Tullinge was disbanded in 1985, the wing painted J35F F18-11 (c/n 35475) in a striking all-red scheme. This aircraft later passed on to *Flygflottilj 10* at Ängelholm, where it continued to fly in its special scheme as F10-11 until it sadly ended up on the F10 dump, despite attempts to rescue it for museum display. *(Author)*

In line with the contemporary trend of 'Going Grey', *Flygvapnet* decided to repaint its updated J35J Drakens in a new air-superiority grey scheme. The first J35J to wear this very smart JA37 Viggen-like two-tone scheme of medium grey upper surface with light grey undersurface and nose was F10-39 (c/n 35539). The Wing number is still yellow (orange on all subsequent aircraft), but the individual code number on wing and fin is painted in high-visibility dayglo orange as an anti-collision measure during normal peacetime training. *(Author)*

SAAB J35J F10-24 (c/n 35624) taxies out for take-off from its home base Ängelholm in southern Sweden. The *'Johan'* modification and refurbishment programme included structural life-time extension, improved LM Ericsson PS-011/A radar reinforced against enemy electronic countermeasures (ECM), an undernose Hughes IR scanner, more effective at low level, various updated avionics, two additional underwing pylons and provision for the more effective Rb74 (AIM-9L Sidewinder) dogfight missile. *(Author)*

SAAB J35J F10-47 (c/n 35588) of 2.div/F10 is towed back to its hangar at the end of the day's flying. *(Author)*

For its primary air defence mission the J35J can carry up to six air-to-air missiles in addition to its single 30 mm Aden cannon mounted in the right wing root. Missiles include the IR homing Rb24J (AIM-9J Sidewinder) and Rb28 (AIM-4D Falcon), as well as the semi-active radar-guided Rb27 (AIM-26B Falcon). All missiles are licence-built in Sweden. SAAB J35J F10-01 (c/n 35601), callsign *Johan Blå 01*, of 2.div/F10, seen here, has an Rb24J on its left inner wing pylon and an Rb27 on its right outer wing pylon. *(Author)*

SAAB J35J Draken F10-24 (c/n 35624), call-sign *Johan Blå 24*, of 2.div/F10 lands at its home base at Ängelholm, loaded up with two IR homing Rb24J Sidewinders on its outer wing pylons, two radar guided Rb27 Falcons on its inner wing pylons and two 525-litre drop tanks on its underfuselage stations. *(Author)*

As it taxies out for take-off from Ängelholm, J35J F10-24 shows its hot end. Repeating the aircraft's individual tail code in large numbers on the wing upper surface is standard *Flygvapnet* practice, used to improve identification during air combat manoeuvring. *(Author)*

Fuelled-up and armed-up ready for flight, J35J Draken F10-07 (c/n 35607) awaits its pilot on the 2nd Division flight-line at F10 Ängelholm. When the decision was taken in 1985 to refurbish and update 67 J35F-2 Drakens to J35J standard, it was originally with the intention of re-equipping all three existing squadrons and setting up an additional fourth Draken squadron within F10. However, since then a general reduction in the number of *Flygvapnet* Wings has resulted in one F10 squadron (1st Division) converting to the AJS37 Viggen and the idea of a fourth F10 squadron being abandoned. So, with only two Draken squadrons remaining at F10 (2nd and 3rd Division), a large number of J35J Drakens became surplus, and these were placed in reserve storage at F9 Säve, near Göteborg, from 1992 onwards. *(Author)*

SAAB J35J Draken F10-01 (c/n 35601), call-sign *Johan Blå 01*, of 2.div/F10 lands at Ängelholm with brake 'chute deployed, airbrakes extended and at a high angle of attack, employing maximum aerodynamic braking, which can reduce the Draken's landing distance to less than 900 m. *(Author)*

SAAB J35J Draken F10-60 (c/n 35584), call-sign *Johan Blå 60*, of 2.div/F10 lands at its Ängelholm base in unusually clean configuration. The special bumper tailwheel became necessary early in the Draken's service history when an engine modification increased the afterburner length. The tailwheel assembly retracts into its own well in concert with the main landing gear, and the tyres are of solid hard rubber. *(Author)*

A pair of light grey 3.div/F10 J35J Drakens, using radio callsigns *Johan Gul 27* and *Johan Gul 43*, lift their noses as they accelerate on take-off from Ängelholm. With full afterburner employed the J35J can take-off in less than 800 m. *(Author)*

A formation take-off by J35J Drakens *Johan Gul 15* and *Johan Gul 57* of 3.div/F10 at Ängelholm. Powered by a 17,200 lb Volvo Flygmotor RM6C afterburning turbofan (a licence-built Rolls-Royce Avon 300 with a Swedish developed Model 67 afterburner), the J35J is capable of more than Mach 2 at high altitude. Average fuel consumption of the Draken is estimated at 3,900 litres per hour, and normal mission duration is 45-60 minutes. *(Author)*

RIGHT & OPPOSITE PAGE:
SAAB J35J Drakens in both new and old colour schemes lined up on the 2nd Division flight-line at Ängelholm. F10 comprises three operational squadrons, of which 1st Division is equipped with AJS37 Viggens and the 2nd and 3rd Divisions operate J35J Drakens. Each squadron consists of some 14–16 aircraft needed to maintain an operational strength of eight combat-ready fighters at any given time, the remaining machines usually undergoing maintenance or being used for training. *(Author)*

Johan Gul 15 and *Johan Gul 57*, J35J Drakens of 3.div/F10, thunder down the runway on take-off from Ängelholm. Note the difference in colours of these two J35Js, F10-15 still in the old two-tone dark green camouflage, while F10-57 has been repainted in the new two-tone light grey scheme. *(Author)*

A J35J with its nosecone removed to reveal its LM Ericsson PS-011/A intercept track/scan radar. Operating in the I/J band this is a simple pulse radar which can illuminate targets for semi-active radar homing missiles. Also visible under the nose is the Hughes-developed S71N infra-red target seeker, which has a range of about 16 miles under normal conditions, making it a useful passive supplement to the radar. Both are fully integrated with the aircraft's SAAB S7B collision-course fire control system. (Author)

OPPOSITE PAGE:
Strapped in and waiting for the take-off signal, the pilot of this J35J Draken is ready to go! The single-piece windscreen provides optimal forward vision, though this is somewhat affected by the weapon sighting system. (Author)

OPPOSITE LEFT:
A 2.div/F10 pilot climbs into his J35J Draken at the start of another mission from Ängelholm. Note the three convex aft-viewing mirrors mounted on the canopy frame to provide the pilot with a limited rear-vision capability. *(Author)*

A J35J pilot of 2.div/F10 prepares for his next mission. The Draken cockpit accommodates a fully automatic SAAB 73SE-F rocket-powered ejection seat that is effective throughout most of the flying envelope down to a speed of 62 mph and zero altitude. The vertically adjustable seat houses the parachute, and has special leg supports and an energy absorbing headrest. A particularly interesting feature of this Swedish seat is that it is angled 30° aft in order to increase pilot tolerance of 'g' forces, an idea that was subsequently adopted many years later by General Dynamics on the F-16. *(Author)*

Compared with today's standards the Draken cockpit is narrow, cramped and rather primitive. The bulged canopy gives an adequate view to the sides, but the view forward is poor because of the weaponry sighting system, and the pilot's view of his vulnerable 'six' is virtually non-existent. *(Author)*

A head-on view of a J35J Draken of *Flygflottilj 10* at Ängelholm. *(Author)*

OPPOSITE PAGE:
This two-seat Sk35C, 35802 F10-81, is equipped with a special spin recovery chute above the engine orifice and is used to train pilots in the superstall phenomenon, a violent and uncontrolled stall that starts with the nose suddenly oscillating up and down at reduced airspeed or too high an angle of attack, and quickly develops into the aircraft falling vertically towards the ground in a stable position with no forward speed at all. The importance of superstall training is emphasised by the fact that almost 20% of *Flygvapnet* Draken crashes are caused by pilots getting into a superstall situation and not being able to recover safely. *(Author)*

Skånska Flygflottilj two-seat Sk35C Draken trainer F10-89 taxies out for take-off from its Ängelholm base. Also known as '*Cäsar*', the Sk35C has no operational capability whatsoever, but is a pure tandem trainer with radar, cannon and underwing pylons removed. *(Author)*

Superstall trainer Sk35C 35802, F16-71, equipped with spin recovery chute, starts its take-off roll at F16 Uppsala, north of the Swedish capital, Stockholm. All Sk35C Draken trainers were operated by the so-called TIS-35 (*Typ Inflygnings Skede 35* or Type Conversion Lead-in 35) at Uppsala from their delivery in 1961-63 until F16 converted to the JA37 Viggen in 1986. At that time the TIS-35 was transferred to F10 Ängelholm, where new Draken pilots continue to receive some 40–50 hours of conversion training on the two-seat Sk35C before moving on to the single-seat J35J fighter. *(Author)*

Four J35F Drakens of 1.div/F10 perform a break after some fine formation flying during an airshow at Ängelholm. *(Author)*

A close-up of the forward fuselage of an F10 Sk35C trainer reveals details of the two-seat cockpit. Special features include a long, heavily sub-framed canopy hinged on the right side, an inner blastscreen mounted between front and rear cockpits, and a periscope to improve the limited forward vision from the back seat. To provide space for the second cockpit some equipment was relocated and the size of the forward fuel tank was reduced, but this was compensated for by extra fuel capacity in the space made available by deletion of the wing root cannon. *(Author)*

Four J35F Drakens of 1.div/F10 manoeuvring in extremely close formation. Note
that the squadron's ghost badge is even
applied to the wing undersides. (Author)

In 1990 the squadrons of F10 flew no fewer than 28 J35F/J Drakens in this impressive formation forming a giant Draken. *(Author)*

A small number of surplus Swedish Drakens have found their way on to the US civil register after retirement from *Flygvapnet* service, all as trade objects in return for museum aircraft relating to Swedish military aviation history. One of them is J35F 35543, which was exchanged for a de Havilland Mosquito NF Mk.XIX in 1988, the deal also involving delivery of three airworthy SAAB 32 Lansens. This Draken has been registered N543J and is operated by Flight Services Inc. at Mojave, California, on various contract work. *(Douglas Sloviak)*

An exceptional view from the 'office' of an RF-35 Draken pilot of *Eskadrille 729*, flying in close formation with his wingman. Note the lines and cross painted on the canopy window, used to position the aircraft relative to the photo-target during reconnaissance missions. *(Flyvevåbnet)*

Draken into NATO

In 1968 the *Kongelige Danske Flyvevåben* (Royal Danish Air Force) became SAAB's first export customer for the Draken, with an order for two squadrons of the specially developed SAAB 35XD (Export Denmark) strike/attack version. This purchase comprised batches of twenty F-35 fighter bombers, twenty RF-35 recce fighters and six TF-35 operational trainers, with designations allocated according to NATO type-nomenclature. A follow-on order was later placed for five additional TF-35 two-seaters, bringing the total *Flyvevåbnet* procurement to 51 Drakens.

Deliveries were made to Karup air base during 1970-72 and 1976-77, with *Eskadrille 725* (ESK or squadron) receiving the fighter variant and *Eskadrille 729* the reconnaissance variant. Trainers were divided equally between both units. All three *Flyvevåbnet* Draken variants were equipped for and fully operational in the fighter-bomber role.

The basic 35XD airframe differed from Swedish Draken versions in many ways, primarily as a result of the Danish optimisation for ground-attack rather than air defence. A general strengthening of aircraft structure was specified to accommodate heavy armament on nine reinforced weapons pylons and a 40% increase in internal fuel capacity. In addition, many electronic systems were modified for compatibility with NATO standards.

To keep up-to-date with modern weapons and avionics technology the *Flyvevåbnet* continually updated its Draken fleet to the latest technical standards. The most extensive modifications have included the MFCD system (modular flare and chaff dispenser) during 1977–80, and the WDNS programme (weapons delivery and navigation system) during 1982–86, the latter providing the Draken with a firing/bombing accuracy equal to, and under visual conditions even better than, many of the modern fighter types such as the F-16A Fighting Falcon.

As a consequence of the general reduction of military forces in both Eastern and Western Europe which took place during the early 1990s, *Flyvevåbnet* decided to retire its Draken fleet without purchasing any replacement aircraft. This meant that *ESK 725* was disbanded by the end of 1991 and *ESK 729* by the end of 1993, thereby putting an end to Draken operations in Denmark and NATO.

A lonely Danish Draken flies down a Norwegian fjord. *Flyvevåbnet* pilots often practise their low-flying skills between the mountains in Norway. *(Flyvevåbnet)*

SAAB F-35 A-006 of *Eskadrille 725* climbs out of Karup after taking off from runway 09R. The aircraft carries empty AERO-3B launcher rails for AIM-9 Sidewinder missiles on its outer wing pylons and empty BM69 practice-bomb racks on its middle and inner wing pylons. *(Steen Hartov)*

An impressive line-up of 41 Danish Drakens (in serial order!) at Karup a few days before Christmas 1991. This was the last chance to arrange such a photograph because *Eskadrille 725* disbanded shortly afterwards, leaving *Eskadrille 729* as the only Draken operator at Karup until that squadron disbanded two years later. At the time the picture was taken, the Danish Draken fleet consisted of 43 aircraft, meaning that only two Drakens are missing from the line-up (due to routine servicing). Of the 51 Drakens delivered, a total of 9 aircraft were lost in accidents (one aircraft crashed after this photo was taken) with the loss of only 3 pilots, an outstanding flying safety record. The Danish Draken fleet logged a total of 143,944 flying hours during their 24 years of service, giving an accident rate of only 0.6 per 10,000 flying hours. For comparison, the Swedish Draken accident rate is about 1.6 per 10,000 flying hours. *(Flyvevåbnet)*

SAAB TF-35 AT-153 of *Eskadrille 725* cruising just above massive cloud cover. This view clearly shows some of the equipment introduced on Danish Drakens during the late 1970s and early 1980s to improve their survivability in a high-threat environment. Modular flare and chaff dispensers are mounted on the rear fuselage immediately in front of the engine orifice (flare dispensers on the fuselage side in continuation of the cooling air intakes, and chaff dispensers under the fuselage next to the arrester hook), and antennas for the ALR-69 radar warning receiver system are mounted on the tip of fin, wings and nose. *(Steen Hartov)*

Low over central Jylland, TF-35 AT-153 breaks right for landing at Karup. Note the extended speed brakes on the rear fuselage above and below the wings. *(Steen Hartov)*

Apparently the man in the back seat of this *Eskadrille 725* TF-35 is not very confident of his driver, judging from the sign he displays, reading 'Help! Careless pilot!' The Danish two-seat Draken retained full operational capability, in contrast to the Swedish Sk35C, which is a pure conversion trainer. Compared to the single-seat F-35, TF-35 modifications included removal of one of the wing-root mounted 30 mm Aden cannon (the left), and a reduced fuel load to make room for the extra seat. Total internal fuel load of the TF-35 was 3,227 litres compared with 4,034 litres for the F-35, but in addition to this both versions usually carried a pair of 1,275-litre drop tanks under the fuselage. *(Steen Hartov)*

Passing the Danish west coast, F-35 A-018 of *Eskadrille 725* heads back towards Karup after a training sortie over the North Sea. *(Steen Hartov)*

A nice shot of a three-ship Draken formation pulling gs in front of Møns Klint, the Danish equivalent of Britain's White Cliffs of Dover. *(Flyvevåbnet)*

41

OPPOSITE PAGE:
Karup-based F-35 A-018 of *Eskadrille 725* climbs high, almost vertical, in full after-burner. This is not a typical situation for the mud-moving Draken fighter-bombers, but a very nice pose for the benefit of the photographer. Pilots and mechanics at Karup quickly learned to love the characteristic double-delta Draken for its simplicity and reliability. It was born back in the 1950s to operate in the harsh Nordic environment, and it was a 'real' flying machine – nothing like the electric jets produced nowadays. *(Steen Hartov)*

SAAB F-35 A-018 of *Eskadrille 725* banks left high in the sky. The Danish F-35 (SAAB designation 35XD) is a special fighter-bomber version of Sweden's J35 air defence fighter, with a strengthened airframe to accommodate heavy ground-attack armament on nine weapons pylons and a 40% increase of internal fuel capacity. Many electronics were also modified for compatibility with NATO standards, including tactical air navigation (TACAN), identification friend or foe (IFF) and a radar warning receiver (RWR), as well as installation of an emergency arrester hook. For weapons delivery, the Swedish intercept radar was replaced by a BT-9 bomb-sight and SAAB 05XDT mission computer. *(Steen Hartov)*

An atmospheric shot of an *Eskadrille 729* RF-35 Draken breaking left into an early winter sunset, showing off its unique double-delta wings to advantage. *(Steen Hartov)*

OPPOSITE PAGE:
A Danish Draken clearly showing off its very large underfuselage drop tanks. These were constructed locally in Denmark to meet a *Flyvevåbnet* requirement of at least 3,000 km range for the SAAB 35XD. Although they seem very similar to the underfuselage drop tanks carried by Swedish J35F/J Drakens, the Danish tanks have a much larger cross-section and hold 1,275 litres each, compared to 525 litres for the Swedish tanks. (In addition, internal fuel capacity has been increased to 4,034 litres on the F-35, compared to 2,865 litres for the J35F/J). Interestingly, Sweden purchased the entire stock of 1,275-litre drop tanks when the Draken was withdrawn from Danish service. *(Steen Hartov)*

During June 1991 a pair of Austrian SAAB 35OE Drakens visited Karup for a local airshow. When departing they took time for some formation flying with a pair of Danish Drakens, as seen in this view. *(Steen Hartov)*

SAAB F-35s A-008, A-009 and A-018 of *Eskadrille 725* practising formation flying. Luckily the Draken never had to demonstrate its firepower in combat, but during exercises it became clear that it was deadly effective in the fighter-bomber role. The Draken could sneak on to its prey alone or in groups, and its small, dark green cross-section was almost impossible to detect when flying at low altitude. Approaching its target head-on at supersonic speed, it could remain undetected until it passed overhead in an ear-splitting roar. *(Steen Hartov)*

A pair of Austrian SAAB 35OE Drakens in formation with specially-painted Danish SAAB F-35 A-009 in its spectacular 1991 Ferrari-red 'Lisbon 725' scheme, flying with wings vertical to show off its underside painting of a gigantic yellow Lindorm. The heraldic shield of *Eskadrille 725* contained the famous dragon from Nordic mythology, the Lindorm, and the squadron motto was *Cave Adsum*, latin for 'Beware, I am here'. *(Steen Hartov)*

Three *Eskadrille 725* Drakens cruise low over central Jylland. Note how well the green camouflage blends in with the background. *(Steen Hartov)*

OPPOSITE PAGE: TOP
SAAB F-35 A-011 of *Eskadrille 725* about to touch down at Karup. With its distinctive double-delta wing and unique bumper tail-wheel, the Draken has often confused local NATO air traffic controllers when an *Eskadrille 725* or *729* pilot on finals radios 'Four greens – no flaps', to confirm that he was approaching in landing configuration! *(Author)*

OPPOSITE PAGE: BOTTOM
SAAB RF-35 AR-113 of *Eskadrille 729* about to touch down on Karup runway 09R. The RF-35 is a fighter/recce version of the basic SAAB 35XD airframe, equipped for and fully operational in both the fighter-bomber and photo-recce roles. Originally five Vinten cameras were mounted in the nose section (45-300 mm lenses), but later the forward-facing camera was replaced by a laser range-finder to improve the aircraft's weapons delivery accuracy in the fighter-bomber role. *(Author)*

Operational trainer TF-35 AT-160 about to touch down on Karup runway 09R. This aircraft was part of a follow-on order for five additional two-seaters delivered to Denmark in 1976-77. Even though Draken production had been closed down and the Linköping assembly-lines were actively engaged in Viggen production, SAAB managed to hand-work these very last Drakens. *(Author)*

Draken A-018 touches down on runway 27L at Karup, specially marked '3,000 hours, F-35, FRO' to celebrate a true world record set on 31 July 1991. On this date Major F.M. Sveistrup (pilot nickname 'FRO') became the first pilot in the world to pass 3,000 flying hours on the SAAB 35 Draken. Congratulations to 'Mr Draken'! *(Author)*

Taking off with its Volvo Flygmotor RM6C
afterburning turbofan in full reheat, F-35
A-012 of *Eskadrille 725* is carrying a pair of
inert AIM-9N Sidewinder missiles on its
outer wing pylons during a visit to CFB
Solingen in Germany. Allied NATO part-
ners often said that an 'alien' fighter lived at
Karup, probably because the Draken's
anatomy looked so different from their own
aircraft. But the Draken keepers and riders
were proud of their wild animal, and for
Danes the tale of the ugly Duckling which
matured into a beautiful Swan is very close
at heart. *(Author)*

During a cold winter's day F-35 A-002 of *Eskadrille 725* touches down on runway 27L at the snow-covered Karup air base. *(Author)*

SAAB TF-35 AT-156 of *Eskadrille 729* is seen touching down on runway 27L at Karup. *ESK 729* used the radio callsign 'Hawkeye' and the squadron's motto was '*Oculus recordaus*', Latin for 'the recording eye'. *(Author)*

A formation take-off by two *Eskadrille 725* F-35 Drakens in very unusual clean configuration, without the almost obligatory pair of 1,275-litre drop tanks. *(Author)*

During a landing roll at Karup, RF-35 AR-119 of *Eskadrille 729* demonstrates the aerodynamic braking which the Draken performs so effectively because of its very large wing area and bumper tailwheel. Both Draken squadrons at Karup were primarily tasked with tactical strike/attack missions, but *ESK 729* undertook a secondary photo-recce role, leaving *ESK 725* as the only full-blooded fighter-bomber unit in *Flyvevåbnet* service, as the F-16 units perform both air defence and strike/attack roles. *(Author)*

SAAB RF-35 AR-101 of *Eskadrille 729* in the matt-green camouflage in which the Danish Drakens were originally delivered. This picture clearly shows how the green paint quickly faded away due to weathering, leaving a more grey-green appearance (at some places even the yellow primer is visible). During the late 1970s this problem was solved by using gloss green paint, which had a much better weather resistance. *(Author)*

Sitting in front of its shelter at Karup, RF-35 AR-115 of *Eskadrille 729* is armed with four LAU-3/A launcher pods, each containing 19 unguided 2.75 in folding fin aircraft rockets (FFAR). In addition to a pair of wing-root-mounted 30 mm Aden cannon, the Danish Drakens can carry a total weaponry load of 9,000 lb on nine hardpoints. Armament includes LAU-3/A rocket pods as well as standard NATO iron bombs such as the Mk.82LD (500 lb Low Drag), Mk.82S (500 lb High Drag, Snakeye 1), Mk.83 (1,000 lb) and Mk.20 (Rockeye) cluster bombs. Until 1982 the powerful but somewhat aged AGM-12B Bullpup air-to-surface missile was employed for anti-shipping operations, but now this role has been taken over by Danish F-16s using AGM-65F Maverick missiles. *(Author)*

SAAB RF-35 AR-117 of *Eskadrille 729* during a visit to Værløse air base outside Copenhagen. The large pod visible under the outer wing contains an ALQ-162 jammer system. *(Author)*

SAAB F-35 A-008 taxies away from its
Eskadrille 725 dispersal at Karup. *(Author)*

A pair of Drakens parked in revetments at Karup. The tubes from the intakes are connected to de-humidifying equipment which very effectively reduces engine corrosion. When parked outside, *Flyvevåbnet* fighters are routinely fitted out with this equipment, which is also known as 'The hoover'. *(Author)*

SAAB TF-35 AT-155 of *Eskadrille 729* awaits its pilots between sorties at Karup. Note the sideways-opening canopy and the windscreen in front of the rear seat, which protects the pilot if the canopy is jettisoned. The small blue bomb on the inner wing pylon is a M/55 practice bomb which contains a smoke marker and weighs only 30 lb but simulates the trajectory of a 500 lb Low Drag bomb. *(Author)*

A technician prepares F-35 A-020 for its next mission from Karup. This view clearly shows the nose-mounted laser rangefinder introduced during 1982-86 as part of the weapons delivery and navigation system update. This modification programme involved the installation of FLIR, HUD, INS and a mission computer, giving the older Draken a firing/bombing accuracy equal to, and under visual conditions even better than, the F-16A Fighting Falcon. *(Author)*

From jet power to muscle power! Having parked his F-35, an *Eskadrille 725* pilot uses a bike to return to the squadron building, which can be a rather long distance at Karup. With two Draken squadrons based at Karup, friendly rivalry was naturally very intense, and *ESK 725* pilots usually referred to their *ESK 729* colleagues as 'chickens' because of the latter's 'Hawkeye' radio callsign. *(Steen Hartov)*

After retirement, many Danish Drakens passed to museums or went to be used for technical training. F-35 A-004 flew for the last time on 2 September 1993, and is now used for aircraft battle damage repair training at Vandel air base. Note that the flare/chaff dispensers around the engine exhaust and the radar warning receiver antenna on the tip of the fin have been removed. This equipment was sold to Austria for installation on their SAAB 35OEs. *(Author)*

SAAB TF-35 AT-158 is the only airworthy Draken remaining in Denmark today. After its last operational flight in *Flyvevåbnet* service on 20 December 1993 it was sold to the Scandinavian Historic Flight and registered OY-SKA. It is maintained at Karup by ex-Draken technicians, but because of financial limitations it is unfortunately very seldom flown. *(Author)*

Today TF-35 AT-153 is flying in the USA as N167TP. After its last operational flight in *Flyvevåbnet* service on 23 September 1993, it was sold to the National Test Pilot School at Mojave, California, together with five other Danish Drakens (AR-110, AR-117, AT-151, AT-154 and AT-157). Another US-based company, Flight Test Dynamics Inc., has similarly acquired Danish Drakens A-020, AR-106, AR-111, AR-116, AR-119, AT-155 and AT-156. *(Author)*

SAAB F-35 'Lisbon 725' (named after the
ESK 725 'Lisbon' radio callsign) at Karup
after its first flight in the striking red colour
scheme which was secretly applied to celebrate the *Eskadrille 725*'s 40th anniversary
on 18 May 1991. Even though the painting
was done without official permission, the
aircraft was allowed to retain its bright red
colours for the rest of that year, though
national insignia and the serial A-009 had to
be applied. *(Author)*

Marking the end of *Eskadrille 725* operations, the pilots who performed the last nine-ship farewell formation on 18 December 1991 parade in front of the squadron's all-red Draken. Officially *ESK 725* was disbanded by 31 December 1991, and exactly two years later, on 31 December 1993, *Eskadrille 729* also disbanded, putting an end to Danish Draken operations. With the disappearance of the Danish Draken, NATO aviation lost an extraordinary fighting machine which always attracted attention when visiting friends around Europe. For the people at Karup, who developed such affection for this perfectly formed piece of metal, the Draken is missed more than anywhere else, but no doubt the special Draken spirit will linger on for many years. *(Steen Hartov)*

Draken under the Northern Lights

In April 1970 the *Suomen Ilmavoimat* (Finnish Air Force) signed a contract for the purchase of 12 SAAB 35XS (Export Suomi) all-weather air-defence fighters for delivery during 1974-75. Based on the Danish 35XD airframe structure and Swedish J35F avionics/weaponry systems, the 35XS (*Ilmavoimat* designation SAAB 35S) was constructed by SAAB in knock-down form for final assembly in Finland by the national aircraft manufacturing company, Valmet OY, at its Kuorevesi facility near Halli.

In addition, Finland acquired several batches of ex-Swedish Drakens, all low-houred airframes from *Flygvapnet* surplus stocks which were refurbished by Valmet OY before being passed on to the *Ilmavoimat*. These deliveries comprised six SAAB 35BS (ex-J35B) in 1972, three SAAB 35CS (ex-Sk35C) and six SAAB 35FS (ex-J35F) in 1976–77, followed by another two SAAB 35CS and 18 SAAB 35FS in 1984–86, whereby the *Ilmavoimat* has accumulated a Draken fleet of 47 aircraft.

Initially Drakens were delivered to *Hävittäjälentolaivue 11* (*HävLLv* or fighter squadron) of the *Hämeen Lennosto* (Häme region Wing) based at Tikkakoski near Jyväskylä in central Finland. Later, *HävLLv 11*

relocated to the extreme north, taking up residence at its present base of Rovaniemi within the *Lapin Lennosto* (Lapland region Wing). In 1984 a second Draken unit was formed as *HävLLv 21* of the *Satakunnan Lennosto* (Satakunta region Wing) at Pirkkala, near Tampere in south-western Finland.

Finnish military activity is still subject to the Second World War peace treaty signed in Paris on 10 February 1947, according to which *Ilmavoimat* total strength is not to exceed 60 combat aircraft (armed with defensive weaponry systems only) and 3,000 men (not including civilian personnel, of which some 1,500 are employed). However, the restriction does not include training versions of front-line fighters or dedicated trainers possessing a secondary tactical mission, such as the Hawk. Consequently, the SAAB 35S and SAAB 35FS interceptors are classified as combat aircraft while the SAAB 35CS two-seaters and SAAB 35BS transition fighters are classified as trainers.

Present long-term planning calls for the Draken to remain in *Ilmavoimat* service until the year 2005, by which time it will have been replaced by the McDonnell Douglas F-18C/D Hornet.

OPPOSITE PAGE:
Ilmavoimat SAAB 35BS Draken DK-202 in a 60-degree climb, wearing the new toned-down markings introduced during the late 1980s. The 35BS, or *'Bertil'* as the type is also known, is powered by a 14,400 lb Volvo Flygmotor RM6B afterburning turbofan (licence-built Rolls-Royce Avon 200 with a Swedish developed Model 66 afterburner), which is not quite as powerful as the 17,200 lb RM6C of the later 35FS and 35S Draken versions. *(Jyrki Laukkanen)*

SAAB 35S DK-207 of *HävLLv 11* from Rovaniemi flies high above a typical Finnish winter landscape of dark forest areas and white ice-covered lakes. Among Finnish personnel the 35S is often affectionately referred to as *'Sigurd'*, continuing the Swedish tradition of giving names starting with the same letter as the type designation. *(Jyrki Laukkanen)*

Of particular interest on the fin of SAAB 35FS DK-259 are the barely visible remains of a very special badge, (the badge can also be found on Draken pilots' helmets and flying suits). This diamond-shaped badge, containing a Draken planform and a single star, is the official badge of the Draken Order, a ceremonial association of Draken pilots from all over the world. The number of stars in the badge indicate the pilot's rank within the Order; one star for Draken Knight, two stars for Draken Master and three stars for Draken Grand Master. The Draken Order was founded on 13 May 1960 at F13 Norrköping in Sweden, and continues to arrange regular meetings at different Draken bases in nations operating the type. To become a member of the honourable Draken Order, candidates must have achieved at least Mach 1.4 and logged a minimum of ten flying hours on the Draken. The purpose of the Draken Order is to worship the Draken 'soul' through different social activities, the nature of which unfortunately remains secret! *(Jyrki Laukkanen)*

SAAB 35FS DK-255 patrols low over massive clouds, armed with live Rb27 Falcon air-to-air missiles. Of the *Ilmavoimat* Draken fleet, only the 35FS and 35S interceptors are classified as combat aircraft, while the 35BS transition fighters and 35CS two-seaters, both types having no real operational capability without weaponry avionics, are considered trainers. *(Jyrki Laukkanen)*

A nice flying shot of SAAB 35FS DK-271 of *HävLLv 21* from Tampere-Pirkkala (note the rare application of a squadron badge on the fin). The long rail on the left underwing pylon is a launcher used for testing the Russian R-3S IR guided air-to-air missile (NATO designation AA-2 Atoll); which is routinely carried by the *Ilmavoimat* MiG-21bis but has also been evaluated on the Draken. *(Jyrki Laukkanen)*

A pleasing air-to-air study of two-seat SAAB 35CS Draken trainer DK-268 over the country of a thousand lakes, which is so beautifully covered by snow during winter. The *Ilmavoimat* has five of these ex-*Flygvapnet* Sk35C *'Cäsar'* conversion trainers in its inventory, and as in Sweden they are not camouflaged but have retained the natural-metal finish. *(Jyrki Laukkanen)*

SAAB 35BS Draken DK-202 cruises over the Finnish countryside. This aircraft was originally delivered to the *Ilmavoimat* on 2 May 1972, and after 21 years of service flew its last operational sortie on 9 September 1993. Because of their age, the 35BSs were the first Finnish Drakens to be retired, and the final mission was flown by DK-206 on 6 October 1995. Interestingly, all six SAAB 35BS Drakens carried individual names inscribed at the top of their fins as follows: DK-202 *'Mikko'*, DK-204 *'Pekka'*, DK-206 *'Hantta'*, DK-208 *'Jussi'*, DK-210 *'Kari'* and DK-212 *'Vihtori'*. *(Jyrki Laukkanen)*

SAAB 35FS DK-269 of *HävLLv 21* from Tampere-Pirkkala banks to port. The Draken is a popular aircraft with *Ilmavoimat* pilots, and its safety record has been excellent, with only one aircraft lost in flying accidents (also one aircraft has been withdrawn from use after suffering extensive damage as result of a generator fire). *(Jyrki Laukkanen)*

Nice shot of SAAB 35FS Draken DK-253 of *HävLLv 21* from Tampere-Pirkkala, appearing in the toned-down markings introduced during the late 1980s. *(Jyrki Laukkanen)*

OPPOSITE PAGE AND THIS PAGE:
SAAB 35FS Draken DK-253 of *HävLLv 21* from Tampere-Pirkkala manoeuvring in the sky. Powered by a 17,200 lb Volvo Flygmotor RM6C afterburning turbofan (licence built Rolls-Royce Avon 300 with Swedish developed afterburner), the 35FS is capable of more than Mach 2 at high altitude. Finnish standard air-to-air weaponry includes Swedish manufactured Rb27/Rb28 Falcon missiles (licence built AIM-26B and AIM-4Ds) and Rb24/Rb74 Sidewinder missiles (licence built AIM-9Js and AIM-9Ls). *(Jyrki Laukkanen)*

ABOVE AND OPPOSITE:
The two fighter types that have constituted the backbone of Finnish air defence during the last two decades are caught in the air together on a rare occasion. SAAB 35FS Draken DK-243 belongs to *HävLLv 21*, based at Tampere-Pirkkala, and MiG-21bis MG-134 is based at Kuopio-Rissala with *HävLLv 31*. Both types will eventually be replaced by the F-18C/D Hornet. *(Jyrki Laukkanen)*

SAAB 35FS Draken DK-231 in an almost vertical dive, photographed from a BAe Hawk. Trying to stay on the wing of a manoeuvring Draken with a Hawk is pretty difficult, owing to the different performance capabilities of the two types. It is almost impossible to stay close and in a good photo position during vertical manoeuvres, as with full power the Draken out-accelerates the Hawk, and when pulling gs the drag produced by the large double-delta wing slows down the Draken quite quickly while the Hawk just keeps going.
(Jyrki Laukkanen)

Four *HävLLv 11* Drakens (three 35Ss and one 35FS) sit on the Rovaniemi flight-line, ready for their next mission. Responsible for airspace surveillance as well as command and control of interceptors in Northern Finland, this unit is situated inside the Arctic Circle and experiences particularly demanding operating conditions during winter, with temperatures often as low as -35 degrees Celsius and perpetual darkness most of the time. *(Author)*

SAAB 35BS DK-210 of *HävLLv 11* being prepared for a mission at Rovaniemi. Note the sub-framed canopy, which does not offer so clear a view as the one-piece canopy of the 35FS/35S. The 35BS carries only one 525-litre drop tank on a central fuselage station. *(Author)*

A ground crewman helps the pilot of SAAB 35S DK-213 to strap in before a mission from Rovaniemi in Lapland. Note the extra missile pylon clearly visible below the inner wing. This has only recently been fitted on Finnish *'Sigurd'* Drakens, and is similar to that included on the Swedish J35J update programme. *(Author)*

SAAB 35S DK-221 taxies out from the Rovaniemi flight-line. This aircraft has undergone the modification programme carried out on the 12 *Ilmavoimat* 35S Drakens in the early 1990s. The programme included the installation of chaff/flare dispensers on the aft fuselage, close to the engine nozzle (as on the Danish F-35 update) and two additional underwing pylons fitted below the inner wings (as in the Swedish J35J version), enabling it to carry six instead of four air-to-air missiles. *(Author)*

A beautiful winter scene showing SAAB 35CS DK-262 taxying out for a training mission. *(Jyrki Laukkanen)*

OPPOSITE PAGE: TOP
Named *'Kreivi von Rosen'* (Count von Rosen) in memory of the Swede who founded military aviation in Finland back in 1918, SAAB 35S Draken DK-223 is operated by *Hävittäjälentolaivue 11* (Fighter Squadron 11), organised within the *Lapin Lennosto* (Lapland Wing) at Rovaniemi. This photo shows the markings used on Drakens before 1990, with large serial and national symbols as well as the squadron badge on the fin. *(Author)*

OPPOSITE PAGE: BOTTOM
SAAB 35FS Draken DK-225 of *Hävittäjälentolaivue 21* (Fighter Squadron 21), organised within the *Satakunnan Lennosto* (Satakunta Wing) at Tampere-Pirkkala, which is responsible for airspace surveillance and command/control of interceptors in south-western Finland. Note again the pre-1990 markings. *(Author)*

DK-247 heads a Draken line-up during the annual *Ilmavoimat* summer shooting camp, where all fighter units deploy to Oulu in Northern Finland for a three-week period to practise air-to-air gunnery against targets towed by Learjets. All of the Finnish single-seat Draken variants are visible in this shot, including the 35FS *'Filip'* (DK-247), 35S *'Sigurd'* (DK-213) and 35BS *'Bertil'* (DK-204). *(Jyrki Laukkanen)*

SAAB 35FS DK-235 taxies out for take-off
from a snow-covered runway. Winter in
Finland is usually extremely cold and harsh,
making it impossible to keep air bases clear
of snow and ice. *Ilmavoimat* aircraft therefore operate from hard-packed snow- or
ice-covered runways as a matter of routine.
(Jyrki Laukkanen)

SAAB 35FS DK-241 lands on a cold winter's day, rolling on its tailwheel and thereby using aerodynamic braking as much as possible to avoid employing wheel brakes at high speeds on the icy runway. *(Jyrki Laukkanen)*

SAAB 35S DK-217 on a snow-covered Finnish air base. All 12 35S Drakens are operated by *HävLLv 11* at Rovaniemi, and are expected to remain in service until the year 2005. The 35S is the only Finnish Draken variant equipped with an IR sensor under the nose, and is the most advanced Draken version in *Ilmavoimat* service, as it has been continually modified and kept up to date. *(Jyrki Laukkanen)*

SAAB 35CS Draken DK-262 of *HävLLv 11* takes off from Rovaniemi for a training sortie over Lapland. Completely lacking operational equipment (no radar, weapons systems or underwing pylons), this relatively light trainer has the highest thrust-to-weight ratio of all Draken versions and is generally regarded as the 'family sports car'. *(Author)*

A pair of SAAB 35BS Draken take off from Rovaniemi on a local training mission over Lapland. Within the *Ilmavoimat* each *Hävittäjälentolaivue* (fighter squadron) comprises two flights with eight to ten Drakens (or MiG-21s), one flight with four to six Hawks (for avanced/operational training) and one flight with single examples of the Piper Arrow, Piper Chieftain and Valmet Redigo (for local liaison and communication). *(Author)*

SAAB 35BS Draken DK-210 returns to Rovaniemi after a training mission. The aircraft carries Rb74 training rounds on the underwing pylons. In *Ilmavoimat* service the *'Bertil'* is only used for training purposes and has very limited operational capability, since most Swedish avionics were removed before delivery (including radar and navigation system) and replaced by a simple radar bearing compass. *(Author)*

SAAB 35FS DK-267 carries the tail badge of the *Ilmavoimien Koelentokeskus* (Air Force Flight Test Centre) based at Halli in south-western Finland. This unit operates single examples of most Finnish aircraft types, and is tasked with the development and evaluation of new equipment and tactics. *(Author)*

SAAB 35S DK-213 of *HävLLv 11* touches down at Rovaniemi after a mission over northern Lapland. *HävLLv 11* will be the last *Ilmavoimat* fighter unit to convert to the new F-18C/D as the Hornet will first replace *HävLLv 21* Drakens and *HävLLv 31* MiG-21s. *(Author)*

SAAB 35FS DK-269 lands with its brake 'chute deployed. It has the pre-1990 high-visibility markings. *(Author)*

SAAB 35S DK-221 of *HävLLv 11* touching down at Rovaniemi after a mission over northern Lapland. The 35S is the most advanced Draken version in *Ilmavoimat* service and it has been continually modified and kept up-to-date with the installation of new and more advanced avionics and weaponry systems. Also a complete overhaul programme has increased the 35S structural airframe lifetime from 1500 to 2700 flying hours. *(Author)*

SAAB 35CS DK-262 of *HävLLv 11* about to touch down at Rovaniemi after a training flight. Note that the two-seat 35CS has no retractable tailwheel but only a small tail bumper, and that the tailcone is shorter than on later Draken models. This is because the Sk35C retained the early RM6B engine and short Model 65 afterburner of the initial production J35A. *(Author)*

In April 1976 Sweden gave a surplus J35A airframe to Finland as a gift. Although it never flew in *Ilmavoimat* service, it was serialled DK-200 and used for ground instructional training at Rovaniemi. *(Author)*

Draken over the Alps

The fourth and final Draken operator is the *Österreichische Luftstreitkräfte* (Austrian Air Force), which only recently became a member of the Draken family. The search for an Austrian all-weather interceptor has been an extremely long process involving some 20 years of political infighting, economical problems and hectic public debate. Finally, in May 1985, a contract was signed for the purchase of 24 ex-Swedish J35Ds converted to SAAB 35OE standard.

SAAB 35OE conversion, carried out by SAAB and FFV Aerotech, comprised very extensive modifications and a complete overhaul which added a further 1000 flying hours to airframes originally constructed in the 1963–65 period.

As had been the case when Denmark and Finland worked up on the Draken, *Flygvapnet* provided an extensive training programme to convert Austrian pilots and technicians on to the 35 system. According to the contract, an initial 24 Austrian pilots were to receive a total of 1800 hr of Draken transition flying in Sweden, which naturally became the responsibility of F10 at Ängelholm. Owing to the lack of two-seat Drakens in Austria, future *Luftstreitkräfte* Draken pilots continued to receive their conversion training on F10 Sk35C trainers in Sweden.

Deliveries of the SAAB 35OE started in late 1987, but initially all Drakens were retained in Sweden for pilot training at Ängelholm. When delivered to Austria in 1988–89 the SAAB 35OE entered service with *1st* and *2nd Staffel* (Squadron), based at Zeltweg and Graz-Thalerhof respectively, of the *Überwachungs Geschwader* (Surveillance Wing) belonging to *2nd Fliegerregiment* (Flying Regiment).

Like Finland, Austrian military forces are restricted by a peace treaty originating at the conclusion of the Second World War, but not signed until 1955. According to this, a maximum of 5000 personnel and 70 defensive combat aircraft are allowed in *Luftstreitkräfte* service. Until very recently there has also been a complete ban on guided missile systems of any kind, but now Austria has extraordinarily been allowed to purchase AIM-9 Sidewinder missiles for its SAAB 35OE Drakens.

At present, no plans have been made public regarding a replacement for the Austrian Draken, but no doubt SAAB hopes to sell Austria the JAS39 Gripen.

OPPOSITE PAGE:
This unusual angle clearly shows the Draken's uniquely designed non-symmetrical oval intakes, which are of the fixed-ramp type with no moving parts, yet function to speeds in excess of Mach 2. Also noteworthy is the slightly outward-angled main landing gear, which permits taxying speeds of over 100 mph on back-country highways. *(Author)*

An Austrian SAAB 35OE Draken flying low over the Sound between Sweden and Denmark during operations from Ängelholm in the summer of 1989, shortly after delivery from SAAB. As had been the case when Denmark and Finland worked up on the Draken, the *Flygvapnet* provided an extensive training package to convert Austrian pilots and technicians on to the 35 systems. According to the sales contract, an initial 24 *Luftstreitkräfte* pilots were to receive a total of 1800 hr of transition training in Sweden, which became the responsibility of F10 at Ängelholm. *(Anders Nylén)*

SAAB 35OE Drakens 12 and 24 fly along the Swedish west coast during operations from F10 at Ängelholm. To accommodate the Austrian personnel during their Draken training programme in Sweden, an interim 4th Division was established within the F10 structure on 1 October 1985, at first without any aircraft but eventually operating up to eight SAAB 35OE when deliveries from SAAB commenced. During the summer of 1989 *Luftstreitkräfte* transition in Sweden was completed and 4.div/F10, also known as the *Österrike Division* (Austrian squadron), disbanded after almost four years of operation, the final 35OE leaving Ängelholm on 7 July 1989. *(Anders Nylén)*

In June 1991 a pair of *Fliegerregiment 2* SAAB 35OE Drakens attended an airshow at Karup in Denmark and took time to fly a mission with *Eskadrille 725*. Here Hauptmann Kowatsch in 08 and Oberleutnant Six in 11 formate with the specially painted F-35 A-009 'Lisbon 725'. *(Steen Hartov)*

Four Swiss F-5E/Fs fly in formation with two Austrian SAAB 35OEs during joint air exercises. *Luftstreitkräfte* Draken pilots practise dissimilar air combat manoeuvring against the Swiss Air Force annually, and they have also flown against fighters from Hungary and Sweden. *(Manfred Sommer)*

Austrian SAAB 35OE Draken during a
training mission on a visit to Denmark.
(Steen Hartov)

SAAB 35OE Draken 14 takes off in full afterburner. The SAAB 35OE has retained the
Volvo Flygmotor RM6C engine of the J35D,
the same powerplant as in the J35F and J35J.
(Wolfgang Hainzl)

A pair of *Fliegerregiment 2* SAAB 35OE
Drakens patrol the airspace of their home
country. *(Manfred Sommer)*

SAAB 35OE Drakens 02 and 04 flying in formation with SAAB 105OE 'Yellow A', painted up in a special 'Tiger' scheme to celebrate the 30th anniversary of the *Jagdbomber Geschwader* of *Fliegerregiment 3* based at Linz-Hörsching.
(Wolfgang Hainzl)

During a deployment to Klagenfurt Airport, SAAB 35OE Draken 13 deploys its brake 'chute to reduce landing roll to an absolute minimum (less than 700 m).
(Wolfgang Hainzl)

A pair of SAAB 35OEs from the *1st Staffel* of the *Überwachungs Geschwader* belonging to *FLR 2* take off from Zeltweg on a local training flight. The runway at Zeltweg has been lengthened by a third to facilitate Draken operations. *(Wolfgang Hainzl)*

During the same Klagenfurt deployment, SAAB 35OE Draken 19 demonstrates aerodynamic braking by rolling on its tailwheel with full up elevons and speedbrakes deployed. *(Wolfgang Hainzl)*

SAAB 35OE Drakens 01 and 18 rotate on take-off from Graz-Thalerhof. Because of its geographical location and size, most of Austria is under civil air traffic control, with several international airline corridors crossing the country. *Luftstreitkräfte* Draken pilots have to comply with this extremely restricted airspace, and only three areas are available for military air combat training. Furthermore, supersonic flying is not allowed below 10,000 m at all, owing to noise limitations. *(Author)*

SAAB 35OE Draken 09 touches down at a snow-covered Zeltweg air base. While the *2nd Staffel* of the *Überwachungs Geschwader* at Graz-Thalerhof concentrates on intercept missions, *1st Staffel* at Zeltweg also performs an additional operational training role. For this purpose Zeltweg houses an advanced 35OE flight simulator derived from an ex-*Flygvapnet* J35D simulator previously used by F4 at Östersund-Frösön in Sweden. *(Wolfgang Hainzl)*

SAAB 35OE Draken 15 lands at Zeltweg. Austrian pilots must have logged at least 500 flying hours, of which 300 must have been on jets (SAAB 105OE) before they can start conversion to the SAAB 35OE. Owing to the lack of two-seat Drakens, *Luftstreitkräfte* pilots continue to gain their initial Draken training (40 flying hours) on *Flygvapnet* Sk35C trainers at F10 Ängelholm in Sweden before moving on to the 35OE at Zeltweg (170 flying hours) and later Graz (fully operational). At present about five new pilots complete Draken training each year. *(Wolfgang Hainzl)*

RIGHT AND BELOW:
Pairs of SAAB 35OE Drakens take off from Graz-Thalerhof. The tail markings of both *FLR 2* Draken units are visible in these shots, 06 carrying the markings of *1st Staffel* and 20 the markings of *2nd Staffel*. The markings do not identify the actual operating unit of individual aircraft, since 01 to 12 carry *1st Staffel* markings and 13 to 24 have *2nd Staffel* markings, but in reality both units draw aircraft as needed from the entire pooled Draken fleet. *(Author)*

SAAB 35OE Draken 18 taxies out for take-off from Graz-Thalerhof, armed with AIM-9P Sidewinder missiles (purchased in 1994 from Sweden, where they are produced under licence with the local designation Rb74) on its underwing pylons. Strangely, Austrian military forces had been prohibited from using guided-missile systems by a peace treaty signed at the conclusion of the Second World War, so *Luftstreitkräfte* pilots originally had to undertake their mission using only the Draken's built-in pair of 30 mm Aden cannon. However, with the ending of the Cold War, Article 13 of the treaty (generally known as the Missile Prohibition) became more relaxed, and because of the nearby Yugoslavian crisis Austria was finally allowed to acquire air-to-air missiles for its Drakens. *(Author)*

SAAB 35OE Draken 01 taxies out at Graz-Thalerhof. Note the flare/chaff dispensers around the engine exhaust and the radar warning receiver antenna on the tip of the fin, purchased from Denmark for installation on the 35OE when this equipment became surplus after retirement of the *Flyvevåbnet* Draken fleet in 1993. *(Author)*

SAAB 35OE Drakens 06 and 20 climb out of Graz-Thalerhof. *Luftstreitkräfte* QRA (quick reaction alert) is regularly rotated between the bases of Graz, Zeltweg and Linz, with either SAAB 35OE or SAAB 105OE aircraft standing by to intercept intruders in Austrian airspace. *(Author)*

Awaiting its pilot between missions at Graz-Thalerhof, SAAB 35OE Draken 06 carries the ghost badge of *1st Division*, F10 Ängelholm, on its tail, having been 'zapped' during one of many deployments to Sweden for pilot training. In addition to regular Draken conversion performed at Ängelholm, three detachments to Vidsel in Northern Sweden have been undertaken by Austrian Drakens for aerial gunnery training during 1990, 1991 and 1993. *(Author)*

The forward fuselage and cockpit area of the SAAB 35OE Draken. The air intakes are several inches from the fuselage side to allow for boundary layer clearance. The intake lips are extremely thin and of composite construction, attached to the aluminium intake tunnels using flush rivets. At the time of development this was several generations ahead of today's composite technology. *(Author)*

SAAB 35OE Draken 12 (c/n 351412) at Graz-Thalerhof. The *Luftstreitkräfte* chose a contemporary three-tone air-superiority grey camouflage scheme for its Drakens, very similar to that of the F-16s but with a black nosecone. Austrian Drakens do not carry their construction numbers on the rear fuselage, which is normal practice in other nations, only the 'last two' digits as tail-code. *(Author)*

OPPOSITE PAGE:
Austrian 35OE pilots average about 100 hours per year, but the aim is to increase this to the same level as for 105OE pilots, which is 120 hours/year. In 1995 the *Luftstreitkräfte* Draken fleet was under-manned, with only 15 operational 35OE pilots, but six new pilots on training in Sweden were expected to become opera-tional during 1996. Note the interesting helmet badges worn by this 35OE pilot preparing for his next mission; the blue/yellow/grey diamond badge of the honourable *Draken Order* and the red/white ghost badge of 1st Division, F10 Ängelholm. *(Author)*

Five SAAB 35OE Drakens lined up on the flightline at Graz-Thalerhof. The basic 35OE modifications carried out by SAAB and FFV Aerotech before delivery to Austria comprised removal of specific Swedish equipment and the installation of new avionics such as VHF-radio, ILS-localiser, VOR/DME and IFF transponders. A complete overhaul programme added a further 1000 flying hours to structural airframe lifetime, and a J35F-type clear-vision canopy replaced the original J35D sub-framed canopy. Otherwise the refur-bished 35OE retained its basic J35D features, including the LM Ericsson PS-03/A inter-cept radar, the SAAB 7A sighting system, the Volvo Flygmotor RM6C engine and a pair of 30 mm Aden cannon. *(Author)*

SAAB 35OE Draken 15 on the flight-line at Graz-Thalerhof, together with SAAB 105OE light fighter/trainers. In *Luftstreitkräfte* service each Draken squadron is allocated four SAAB 105OEs for training and target flying, as well as a pair of Cessna L-19 Bird Dogs for communication and liaison flying. *(Author)*

The large day-glo orange numbers clearly visible on this view of SAAB 35OE Draken 10 were introduced in Austria during the early 1990s. It is an old Swedish idea which eases identification of friend/foe during ACM training (air combat manoeuvring) and improves flying safety. In wartime the high-visibility numbers would be removed. *(Author)*

SAAB 35OE Draken 05 from the *1st Staffel* of *FLR 2* taxies out of the new drive-through Quick Reaction Alert shed at its Zeltweg home base. *(Wolfgang Hainzl)*

A front view of an *FLR 2* SAAB 35OE Draken at Zeltweg, well illustrating the exceptionally low frontal area of the basic Draken configuration. Note that refuelling of the Draken takes place through the port under-carriage bay. *(Wolfgang Hainzl)*

Five SAAB 35OE Drakens rest in the woods at Graz-Thalerhof. *(Author)*

Hauptmann Doro Kowatsch immediately after shutdown upon arriving at Karup in Denmark in SAAB 35OE Draken 08 for a local airshow. Kowatsch is one of the most experienced Draken pilots in Austria, as he was among the first *Luftstreitkräfte* pilots undergoing Draken training in Sweden. This first group consisted of three squadron commanders who began Draken conversion training at F10 Ängelholm in January 1986, followed by three instructors in September 1986 and three groups of six operational pilots during 1987–89. Each pilot received 50 hours of standard *Flygvapnet* TIS-35 conversion training on Swedish Sk35C two-seaters and Austrian 35OE fighters, while instructors and commanders performed an additional 75 hours and 125 hours respectively of advanced and tactical flying training on Sk35Cs/J35Fs/35OEs. *(Author)*

SAAB 35OE Draken 04 taxies out for take-off
from RAF Waddington. During early
summer 1995 the *Luftstreitkräfte* deployed
ten Drakens with 12 pilots and 60
supporting personnel to this UK base for a
three-week period, in order to make use of
the North Sea air-combat manoeuvring
instrumentation range. *(Peter Foster)*

SAAB 35OE Draken 03 taxying out for take-
off from Bratislava in Slovakia during a local
airshow in 1994. *(Cor van Gent)*

SAAB 35OE Draken 24 during a refuelling stop at Norvenich in Germany, on its way to RAF Waddington in the UK for a North Sea air-combat manoeuvring instrumentation deployment. The aircraft carries an AIM-9P Sidewinder training round on its right underwing pylon. *Luftstreitkräfte* pilots are not able to practise Sidewinder missile firing in Austria because there are no missile firing ranges in the country; only two ranges for air-to-ground gunnery training. Draken pilots therefore have to qualify for the missile system during deployments abroad, primarily to northern Sweden. *(Lutz Tonne)*

SAAB 35OE Draken 08 being refuelled at Karup in Denmark after arriving for a local airshow in 1991. *(Author)*

Winter scenery on the Zeltweg Draken flight-line. The J35D airframes selected for conversion to 35OE standard in 1987-89 had originally been constructed by SAAB in the 1963–65 period, and had logged an average of 2000 flying hours in *Flygvapnet* service with F4 at Östersund-Frösön and F21 at Luleå-Kallax. Contracturally, they were bought back by SAAB, refurbished and converted in a process requiring 20,000 working hours per airframe, and sold to Austria. *(Wolfgang Hainzl)*

SAAB 35 Draken production

Type	Construction number	Serial	No	Remarks
	Sweden
A/B/D/F prototype	35-1 to 35-9		9	New-built
D/F prototype	35-10 to 35-13		(4)	Modified J35A/B, original c/ns: 35082, 35275, 35081, 35013
J35A	35001 to 35090		90	New-built
J35B	35201 to 35273		73	New-built
C prototype	35800		(1)	Modified J35A, original c/n: 35010
Sk35C	35801 to 35825		(25)	Modified J35A, original c/ns: 35035, 35040, 35038, 35016, 35006, 35007, 35022, 35009, 35008, 35019, 35017, 35020, 35012, 35031, 35005, 35015, 35021, 35032, 35029, 35036, 35030, 35024, 35037, 35033, 35034
J35D	35274 to 35393		120	New-built
E prototype	35901		(1)	Modified J35D, original c/n: 35278
S35E	35902 to 35931		30	New-built
S35E	35932 to 35960		(29)	Modified J35D, original c/ns: 35310, 35288, 35282, 35289, 35302, 35296, 35287, 35297, 35284, 35294, 35283, 35303, 35276, 35299, 35291, 35301, 35279, 35295, 35286, 35300, 35290, 35293, 35298, 35280, 35292, 35277, 35285, 35281, 35274
J35F-1	35401 to 35500		100	New-built
J35F-2	35501 to 35630		130	New-built
J35J	35502, 35512, 35513, 35518, 35520, 35521, 35522, 35524, 35531, 35532, 35533, 35537, 35539, 35540, 35541, 35544, 35545, 35546, 35553, 35554, 35556, 35564, 35565, 35569, 35570, 35572, 35575, 35576, 35577, 35578, 35580, 35582, 35584, 35585, 35586, 35588, 35589, 35590, 35594, 35595, 35596, 35598, 35599, 35601, 35602, 35604, 35605, 35606, 35607, 35608, 35610, 35611, 35612, 35613, 35615, 35616, 35617, 35618, 35619, 35620 35621, 35623, 35624, 35625, 35626, 35627, 35630		(67)	Modified J35F-2, original c/ns retained

SAAB 35 Draken production

Type	Construction number	Serial	No	Remarks
Denmark				
F-35	351001 to 351020	A-001 to A-020	20	New-built
RF-35	351101 to 351120	AR-101 to AR-120	20	New-built
TF-35	351151 to 351161	AT-151 to AT-161	11	New-built
J35F	35420, 35552		[2]	Spares source
S35E	35906, 35922, 35925 35929, 35931		[5]	Spares source
Finland				
SAAB 35BS	35265, 35261, 35245, 35214, 35243, 35257	DK-202 to DK212 (even numbers)	(6)	Modified J35B, original c/ns retained
SAAB 35CS	35823, 35820, 35803, 35807, 35812	DK-262 to DK-270 (even numbers)	(5)	Modified Sk35C, original c/ns retained
SAAB 35FS	35417, 35425, 35481, 35416, 35443, 35444, 35446, 35447, 35448, 35450, 35451, 35441 35455, 35458, 35462, 35483, 35487, 35499, 35460, 35412, 35489, 35449, 35445, 35493	DK-225 to DK-271 (odd numbers)	(24)	Modified J35F-1, original c/ns retained
SAAB 35S	351301 to 351312	DK-201 to DK-223 (odd numbers)	12	New-built
J35A	35026	DK-200	[1]	Ground instructional airframe
J35B	35252		[1]	Spares source
SAAB 35BS	35266	DK-942	[1]	Ground instructional airframe
Austria				
SAAB 35OE	351401 to 351424	01 to 24	(24)	Modified J35D, original c/ns: 35313, 35314, 35315, 35317, 35323, 35324, 35328, 35335, 35336, 35338, 35340, 35341, 35342, 35347, 35351, 35360, 35368, 35370, 35373, 35378, 35382, 35384, 35386, 35393

Total production: 615 new-built (180 modifications)

A line-up of SAAB 35 Drakens from three different nations; an Austrian SAAB 35OE (ex-J35D), a Finnish SAAB 35FS (ex-J35F-1) and a Swedish J35J (ex-J35F-2). *(Author)*

Pilots preparing for a TIS-35 training mission from F10 Ängelholm. *(Author)*